DUBLIN THEN AND NOW

LUCY JOHNSTON

DUBLIN

THEN AND NOW

GILL AND MACMILLAN

Published in Ireland by
Gill and Macmillan Ltd
Goldenbridge
Dublin 8
with associated companies in
Auckland, Delhi, Gaborone, Hamburg, Harare,
Hong Kong, Johannesburg, Kuala Lumpur, Lagos, London,
Manzini, Melbourne, Mexico City, Nairobi,
New York, Singapore, Tokyo
© Photographs, Lucy Johnston 1989
© Text, Gill and Macmillan 1989
Designed by Peter Larrigan
0 7171 1698 0
Print origination by The Type Bureau, Dublin
Printed in Great Britain by The Bath Press, Bath

Introduction

This is a pictorial record of continuity and change in Dublin over the last hundred years or so. By placing new photographs alongside old ones taken from roughly the same angle, one can see at a glance the salient features of the city's development in that time.

I say 'roughly the same angle' because while my brief was to get as close as possible to the position of the original photographer, it was in some cases physically impossible to do so. In other cases, it was simply undesirable. It can be boring to be stuck with someone else's camera angles, so on occasion I rebelled and did my own variation on the theme!

On the whole, I have found that taking these photographs has been a rather depressing experience. It's not that modern Dublin is obviously as awful as late nineteenth-century and early twentieth-century Dublin. It's not. We can all applaud the clearance of the worst slums, the closing of the brothels, the enormous improvement in public hygiene and sanitation. But at least Dublin then was all of a piece. Its core, between the canals, was pretty much as its eighteenth-century builders had left it. It was a unity and it was all there, albeit decayed. Dublin now has much to recommend it but that old unity is gone and no new unity has replaced it. Much of Dublin now is a city of gaps, of half-built sites, a boom town where the money ran out half way through the spree.

It's this provisional, half-finished quality that I found dispiriting about Dublin now. Moreover, those parts of the Georgian centre or the Victorian suburbs which have survived largely unchanged remain the most attractive areas of the city. The twentieth century has swept away the worst excesses of Dublin then, but its positive contribution has been less than one would expect. So much of our modern architecture is just bad modern architecture. I think it a shame that our time – for all its energy and civic improvement – has not made a more lasting architectural contribution to Dublin.

Looking back at these photographs of Dublin then and now laid side by side, I think the most striking change is that caused by trees. Compared with the modern city, Victorian and Edwardian Dublin seemed almost treeless. O'Connell Street is as good an example as any other. The older view is that much harsher and clean-edged without the screen of plane trees that dominates my photographs. Time and again this recurs, emphasised by the fact that most of my photographs were taken in high summer when the trees were in full foliage. Yet their effect seems to me so pervasive that if I were asked to nominate the single biggest change between Dublin then and now, I'd say: trees.

The photographs of Dublin then are nearly all taken from the Lawrence Collection in the National Library of Ireland. This huge collection of over 40,000 images is the biggest single photographic source for Irish life between 1980 and 1910. Although named for William Lawrence who commissioned them for his photographic business, they are in fact the work of his chief assistant, Robert French. I am grateful to the staff of the National Library for their invaluable help.

Finally, I want to thank Gerard Siggins and Michael Pigott who researched and wrote the captions.

Lucy Johnston
Dublin
September 1989

DUBLIN

THEN AND NOW

Sackville (now O'Connell) Street

The building of Carlisle (now O'Connell) Bridge in 1794 led to the widening of Sackville Street two years later. Previously called Drogheda Street (1728) after the Earl of Drogheda, Henry Moore. The General Post Office was opened in 1818, and to its left is the Metropole Hotel with its white-painted iron work. The statue of Sir John Gray, the initiator of the Vartry water supply, had stood there since 1879. Looming in the background is Nelson Pillar erected in 1808. The statue, by Thomas Kirk, was destroyed by an IRA explosion in 1966. The head is preserved in the Civic Museum, South William Street.

Whatever one might think of Nelson Pillar as a public monument, its destruction was typical of that juvenile love of blowing things up and burning things down which has had such a strong appeal to our more inadequate and pathetic 'patriots' for so long. Although never the physical heart of Dublin, the Pillar was certainly the emotional and sentimental centre.

In the course of the present century, O'Connell Street has, in a sense, changed without changing. It is no more fashionable now, relative to the Grafton Street area, than it was then and while it is easy to

deplore the plethora of fast food joints and
'amusement arcades' which give the street an
unnecessarily tatty appearance, things have certainly
improved since late Victorian times when the
pavement on the north side of the street was reserved
at night for prostitutes and their clients. In a physical
and symbolic sense, it remains Dublin's main street,
but in these senses only. It is not the centre of a
fashionable area. Its social life is strangely attenuated:
there are two cinemas but only one pub and very few
restaurants other than those of the fast food variety. In
short, it is not the sort of street where people
congregate in the evenings in public in a gregarious,

*O'Connell Bridge and
O'Connell Street*

socialising atmosphere. O'Connell Street in the
evenings is generally full of people going somewhere
else.

The second pair of photographs show O'Connell
Bridge and O'Connell Street from the top of Carlisle
Buildings (old photograph) and its 1960s replacement,
O'Connell Bridge House. The difference in height of
the two buildings is evident from the contrast.
Carlisle Buildings was an undistinguished building,
but at least it was in scale with its surroundings.
O'Connell Bridge House is equally undistinguished
and quite out of scale. Still, the view from the top is
nice …

Gresham Hotel

Destroyed during the civil war in 1922, the original Gresham Hotel had been opened in 1817 by Mr Thomas Gresham. In 1833 Gresham, who lived in Kingstown (now Dun Laoghaire), was presented with a silver salver in recognition of his leading role in opening the extension to the Kingstown Railway.

The modern hotel is a pleasing piece of architecture which dominates the north side of O'Connell Street without overwhelming it. It is certainly a more successful building than the rather conventional nineteenth-century structure which it replaced. It is very much a building of the 1920s, modern in concept, with hints of the Egyptian motifs then in vogue.

Gresham Hotel

The Rotunda

The Rotunda Hospital, designed by Richard Cassells and founded by Dr Bartholomew Mosse, was the first lying-in hospital in Great Britain or Ireland. Originally in a lane off George's Street, it was moved to its present site in 1757. In order to provide an income for the hospital, pleasure gardens were opened and in 1767 the Rotunda room was built. Concerts, entertainments, balls and suppers were held here, making it the social centre of the capital. The triangular obelisk, commemorating Charles Stewart Parnell, was unveiled in October 1911 by John Redmond, leader of the Irish Parliamentary party.

Bartholomew Mosse was the son of a clergyman and began his medical career as an army surgeon. He transferred to midwifery and it was his experience of the utterly wretched conditions in which the poor of Dublin gave birth that prompted him to found the Lying-In Hospital.

The Rotunda has maintained its position as one of the outstanding architectural features of the north inner city, a part of Dublin that has suffered a continuing decline in the course of the twentieth century.

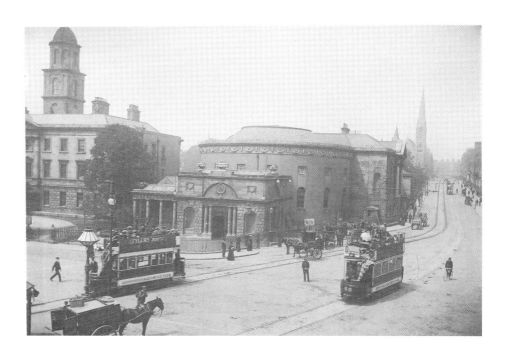

The Rotunda

Rotunda Hospital and Gardens

Laid out as pleasure gardens in the 1750s, the income derived from admission prices was used to fund the hospital. Shady walks and groves, a tea shop, bandstand and bowling green were installed, and if the weather was inclement the gentility promenaded in the Rotunda. The gardens went out of fashion by the second decade of the nineteenth century and fell into decay. By the 1890s tennis courts were in use by hospital staff, and nowadays the area has been used to build several hospital ancillary buildings, a nurses' home and the Garden of Remembrance on the northern end.

Rotunda Hospital and Gardens

Liberty Hall

At ten-to-twelve on Monday 24 April 1916, James Connolly led 28 men and eight boys out of Liberty Hall and set off to take on the British Empire. Jim Larkin's Irish Transport and General Workers' Union had been based there since 1912. The building was badly damaged by shelling during Easter Week but was eventually restored before being demolished in the 1950s. The present Liberty Hall is the second tallest building in Ireland.

The old Liberty Hall building dated from the 1820s and while it had no architectural distinction it was at least in scale with its surroundings. The modern building is, however, two hundred feet and totally out of scale with everything around it. It was Dublin's first 'skyscraper' and its building aroused much enthusiasm and excitement in the heady years of the mid 1960s. It is, however, a particularly unfortunate example of the architecture of that period, bad examples of which are to be found all over Dublin.

Liberty Hall

Amiens Street Station

The railway station at Amiens Street was built between 1844 and 1846. Gateway for travellers to the north side of Dublin, it was renamed Connolly Station after James Connolly. The street is named after Viscount Amiens, Earl of Aldborough, whose home Aldborough House is nearby.

At the turn of the century, the Amiens Street area was on the edge of the Monto Town, Dublin's notorious red light district. In *Ulysses,* Buck Mulligan, Stephen Dedalus, Bloom and the medical students disembark from a loopline train at Amiens Street in order to make their way to the nearby kips. The kips disappeared in the 1920s, but Mabbot Lane, the access route which they took on their way to Nighttown, is still visible on the right-hand side of Talbot Street going up towards O'Connell Street.

While the worst features of this area have been swept away, it has none the less remained fairly dilapidated and Amiens Street itself is a rather sad architectural hotchpotch. However, the building of the new financial services centre at nearby Custom House Quay may be a focus for the future regeneration of the whole area.

Amiens Street Station

Grafton Street

Grafton Street got its name from Henry Fitzroy, First Duke of Grafton, who was the illegitimate son of Charles II by the Duchess of Cleveland. Grafton Street was first laid out towards the end of the seventeenth century, although the first printed reference to it occurs in a statute of 1708. In its early years, it stood at the eastern limit of the city in what was an unfashionable quarter. But the construction of Leinster House in the 1740s was the first decisive movement in shifting the centre of fashionable life in Dublin from the north to the south side. From the mid eighteenth century onward, Grafton Street became

part of the *beau monde* of Dublin. John Rocque's map
of 1756 already shows the surrounding streets —
Duke Street, Anne Street, Dawson Street and
Molesworth Street — laid out.

Grafton Street consolidated its fashionable
reputation in the nineteenth century by becoming the
city's premier shopping street, a position it has held to
the present day. In *Ulysses*, 'Grafton Street, gay with
housed awnings' lured the senses of Mr Bloom. For
most of the twentieth century, it remained relatively
unchanged. In the 1950s its genteel atmosphere was
epitomised by the respectable ladies providing piano

Grafton Street

and violin accompaniment to afternoon tea in Robert Roberts café at No. 44. However, then and now, its most famous café is Bewley's, which stands on the site of White's Academy, a famous eighteenth-century school where the future Duke of Wellington, among others, was educated. Along with its sister cafés in Westmoreland Street and South Great George's Street, Bewley's is one of the great Dublin institutions.

Grafton Street managed to survive the depredations of the 1960s and '70s very well. The building and property boom of those years saw many fine traditional Dublin buildings being replaced by what were for the most part modern buildings of little or no distinction and in some cases of outstanding ugliness. Happily, Grafton Street was left untouched by most of

this. Indeed, the most innovative development in those years was the experimental pedestrianisation of the street in the summer of 1971. To the immense disappointment of many people, this arrangement was not made permanent and the street was soon returned to traffic. However, the proposals for pedestrianisation were taken up in earnest again in the mid 1980s and Grafton Street is now completely pedestrianised. More than any other twentieth-century development, pedestrianisation has fundamentally changed both the physical appearance of the street and its atmosphere. The street has been completely repaved and now has a distinctly continental atmosphere, especially in summer.

St Stephen's Green

Granted to the people by the brewing Guinness family, this view of the main entrance at the top of Grafton Street features a memorial to Irish soldiers who died fighting with the British army in the Boer War.

St Stephen's Green was originally common land which was first enclosed in the 1660s. The west side of the Green, seen in these photographs, was a traditional place of execution: a gibbet stood on the site now occupied by the Royal College of Surgeons in Ireland. Because of this, the west side of the Green developed more slowly and, with the one exception of the College of Surgeons, never scaled the architectural heights of the other three sides. None the less, the old photograph shows a pleasing clutter of buildings. The twentieth century, regrettably, has not been kind to this side of Stephen's Green. In particular, the area between the College of Surgeons and South King Street has for years been run-down and neglected, although the process of redevelopment has recently begun with the opening of the upmarket Stephen's Green Shopping Centre.

St Stephen's Green

Shelbourne Hotel

Built in 1866, there has been very little subsequent change to the exterior. It was occupied by the crown forces in 1916 to put pressure on the insurgents in the College of Surgeons. Six years later, a room in the hotel was used by those drafting the constitution of the new state.

The Shelbourne stands on the north side of St Stephen's Green, the first side to be developed. Kerry House originally stood on this site. It was the town house of Thomas Fitzmaurice, the First Earl of Kerry. On his death it passed to his son, the First Earl of Shelburne, and then to his second son, the Hon. Thomas Fitzmaurice. When Fitzmaurice died in the late eighteenth century a Mr Luke White bought Kerry House. He leased it to the army as a troop billet until in 1818 one of the soldiers accidentally started a fire which burnt the place down. White rebuilt it with the government compensation money and leased three of the new houses to one Martin Burke who opened a hotel. Burke died in 1863 and his family sold the hotel to a syndicate which bought two adjoining houses, demolished Burke's hotel, and replaced it with the splendid building which still stands there, dominating this corner of St Stephen's Green.

Shelbourne Hotel

University College, Earlsfort Terrace

The building was the venue for Dublin International Exhibition, held here in 1865, and later became the Royal University. The campanile on the right was later moved to Kildare Street as a chimney for government buildings. The new front to the university was added in 1915. The three statues over the pediment now grace the small park beside the City Hall.

In one of the most regrettable moves of the last twenty years, University College moved its main campus from this splendid city centre site to the suburban fastness of Belfield. It thus weakened the link between town and gown which is so much a feature of the best European universities, conforming instead to an American model. However, UCD's removal to the suburbs did have one outstandingly beneficial effect in that the old *Aula Maxima* in Earlsfort Terrace was converted into the National Concert Hall. The panache with which this was done has been a legitimate source of pride to Dubliners, not least because the absence of a proper venue for the performance of serious music had for many years been a scandal in the city with pretensions to being a cultural capital.

University College,
Earlsfort Terrace

Merrion Square

Was it on this tram that James Joyce came to town on that warm summer day, 16 June 1904? He hoped to see Nora Barnacle who worked in Finn's Hotel just a few yards away. The north side of Merrion Square at this time was mostly populated by members of the medical profession. Eighty years on, there have been very few apparent changes to the house fronts or the street furniture.

Merrion Square was developed by the Sixth Viscount Fitzwilliam, the great eighteenth century developer of Dublin's Georgian south side. The architect was John Ensor who was also employed on the Gardiner estate on the other side of the city. In the mid eighteenth century, the north side was more fashionable than the south side and the Gardiner estate — centred on Mountjoy Square — had the great advantage of occupying rising ground. Merrion Square and its neighbour Fitzwilliam Square had, however, an even greater advantage — the proximity of Leinster House and the magnetic pull which the residence of the Duke of Leinster had for leaders of fashion. The original development of Merrion Square was not only a triumph of architecture but also of civil engineering, because the north side was exposed to the tidal inundations of the Liffey which used to come this far south prior to the extension eastward of the south quays.

By the late eighteenth century, however, all that was forgotten and Merrion Square had become what it was to remain for over a century: the most desirable address in Dublin.

Merrion Square

Leinster Lawn and Merrion Square

The statue on the right in the old photograph is of Prince Albert, husband of Queen Victoria. The statue was moved towards the right-hand side of the photograph next to the Natural History Museum shortly after the foundation of the state. The present monument was erected to the memory of Cathal Brugha, Michael Collins and Kevin O'Higgins in the 1920s.

*Leinster Lawn and
Merrion Square*

Masonic Hall and Leinster House

James Fitzgerald, Earl of Kildare and later Duke of
Leinster, built his magnificent mansion in fields
outside the city in 1745. The Royal Dublin Society
bought it in 1914 for £10,000. Some of the earliest
Dublin Horse Shows were held here before 1881 when
the event was moved to Ballsbridge. To the left of the
photograph is the Masonic Hall (1868), which houses
masonic regalia once used by Daniel O'Connell. This
street, Molesworth Street, has seen very little change
except for the removal of the high wall and gate on
Leinster House.

Molesworth Street was laid out in 1795 by John,
Second Viscount Molesworth. The western end of the
street, nearest Dawson Street, has been extensively
rebuilt in the last twenty years but the eastern end
towards Kildare Street, seen here, survives very much
as it was.

*Masonic Hall and
Leinster House*

Mount Street Bridge

Crossing the Grand Canal, Mount Street Bridge was the scene of a celebrated action during the 1916 rising. A detachment from Eamon de Valera's Boland's Mill garrison successfully held up British reinforcements who were making their way from Kingstown (Dun Laoghaire) to the city centre. The old photograph shows the scene in the aftermath of that affray.

Mount Street Bridge dates from the late eighteenth century and, as with all the bridges on the Grand Canal, it marks the limit of eighteenth-century Georgian development. The Georgian style survived in Dublin well into the nineteenth century, having been abandoned everywhere else but its classic Dublin phase ends on the line of the Canal.

Lower Mount Street was transformed in the building and redevelopment boom of the 1960s and is, regrettably, a very poor advertisement for that 'Gung Ho' decade. True, the original Georgian houses had become shabby and neglected. Yet their wholesale clearance in favour of a series of utterly undistinguished office buildings was a great loss to the city. In particular, little regard was shown to Lower Mount Street's important position as one of the principal approaches to Merrion Square.

Mount Street Bridge

Foster Place

Named after the last speaker of the old Irish House of Commons John Foster (1740-1828). Across Dame Street can be seen the old head office of the Hibernian Bank, now subsumed into the Bank of Ireland. The equestrian statue of William III stands in the middle of the street with its tail to TCD. Much reviled by the citizenry, and several times blown up, it was finally taken down in 1929. Some panels from around the plinth are preserved in the Dublin Civic Museum nearby.

Foster Place itself has hardly been changed at all by the passage of time, dominated as it is by the old Bank of Ireland head office on one side and the former head office of the Royal Bank of Ireland (now part of Allied Irish Banks) on the other. The former offices of the Central Bank of Ireland enclose the street at the northern end.

Foster Place

Dame Street

The Wide Streets Commissioners, appointed in 1757, were responsible for the fine broad streets we see in the capital today. The statue of Grattan by Foley was erected in 1876 across the road from the Old Parliament House.

Dame Street takes its name from a church, dating back to at least the twelfth century, called 'Sainte Marie del Dam', the 'Dam' in question being a mill-dam which stood beside it. The word 'Dam' was gradually corrupted to 'Dame'. In 1488 Sir Richard Edgecombe, who had been dispatched from England by King Henry VII to meet with the Earl of Kildare, did so in 'the church called Our Lady of the Dames'. The church stood on Cork Hill, which was at the edge of the medieval town, and it later gave its name to the thoroughfare which connected the old town and Hoggen Green (later College Green).

Dame Street has retained the commercial character which it established in Victorian times. It is now dominated by the new headquarters of the Central Bank of Ireland, a building that aroused enormous controversy at the time of its construction. It is, however, a very remarkable piece of architecture — one of the finest in Dublin — although not perhaps situated in the most appropriate position.

Dame Street

Dublin Castle

The lower yard of Dublin Castle, seat of British power in Ireland since the twelfth century. It now houses the State Apartments used on formal state occasions such as the inauguration of Presidents of Ireland. The Lower Castle Yard, pictured here, houses the Chapel Royal *(left)*.

The present Castle buildings are mainly a creation of the eighteenth century and after, but a fortified post has stood on this site since 1204, when building began on the orders of King John. It stood at the eastern end of the medieval city on the edge of the Hill of Dublin. Despite its symbolic military importance, it was allowed to fall into an alarming state of neglect over many years until the restoration work of the eighteenth century. For generations of Irish nationalists, it was the supreme symbol of British rule in Ireland, the first and last bastion of colonial rule.

In addition to its ceremonial functions, the Castle now houses a number of government departments, not least the offices of the Revenue Commissioners, whose rule is sometimes felt by the citizenry to be at least as onerous as that of the long-departed British!

Dublin Castle

Ship Street Barracks

The barracks are at the back of Dublin Castle and were evacuated after the Anglo-Irish Treaty in 1922. Visible above the buildings in the modern photograph is the top of the controversial Dublin Civic Offices built on the site of the Viking settlement at Wood Quay.

Ship Street Barracks

St James's Hospital,
James's Street

St James's Hospital, James's Street

Formerly the South Dublin Union, no street frontage in Dublin has changed as dramatically as this. In the modern photograph, only the building shaded by the tree *(extreme right)* is a partial survival from the grim old SDU. It is also visible on the extreme right of the old photograph. The detailed modern photograph of the old section highlights the continuity. But apart from that, the SDU frontage has been swept away, leaving nothing but open space and access points for cars and ambulances.

Dining Hall, Royal Hospital

The Royal Hospital, Kilmainham, was built on the orders of King Charles II and the first stone was laid by his viceroy, the Duke of Ormond, in 1680. The Dining Hall – measuring 100 by 50 feet – was copiously decorated by relics of past battles and wars. The RHK was inhabited at its peak by over 300 retired soldiers.

The Royal Hospital was modelled on Les Invalides in Paris and the Chelsea Hospital in London. Indeed, for many years its residents were known colloquially as 'Chelsea Pensioners'. Once it ceased to be used as a home for old soldiers, it became a repository for many items belonging to the National Museum for which storage space was unavailable in the main museum building in Kildare Street. In particular, the statue of Queen Victoria which used to stand outside Leinster House facing down Molesworth Street, has been moved there.

The Royal Hospital has been the subject of a magnificent restoration in recent years, evidence of which is plainly visible in these photographs. It has become one of the city's most valuable cultural resources, as a venue for concerts, banquets, exhibitions and other events.

Dining Hall,
Royal Hospital

St Patrick's Park

Built in 1900 just a few years before the older photograph was taken, it replaced the festering slums and yards that huddled around the cathedral. Financed by the Guinness family, the Iveagh Trust buildings still remain a model of this type of housing.

St Patrick's Park

Weavers Square

Not all of the French Huguenots who settled in Dublin were weavers, but those that were settled in the area of the Coombe, building their distinctive high-gabled houses like these in Weavers Square. They became quite prosperous, but by the middle of the nineteenth century the trade began to decline. The last of the weaver-type houses were demolished in the 1950s.

Weavers Square

Ardee Street

One of the many names in this area of Dublin connected with the Earl of Meath. Granted to Sir William Brabazon in 1545, the lands outside the walls of the city eventually developed as an industrial centre. Ardee Street, originally called Crooked Staff, formed one boundary of the Earl of Meath's 'liberty'. By one hundred years ago, however, the street had fallen on hard times and mostly contained decaying tenements. One exception was the brewery of Thomas Watkins which eventually closed in the 1930s.

Ardee Street

St James's Church

Built in 1861 to replace an earlier church. The graveyard, lately cleaned up, contains the impressive tomb of Sir Toby Butler, who framed the Articles of the Treaty of Limerick of 1691. The spire was taken down when the church finally closed in 1963. The gateway on the right with the military insignia was the entrance to the 'Military Infirmary for the care of the sick and wounded of His Majesty's Army in the Kingdom', erected in 1730.

St James's Church

Marshalsea Lane

This lane, off Thomas Street, led to the Marshalsea Debtors' Prison. Insolvent debtors were incarcerated here in the eighteenth and nineteenth centuries, often together with their families, in dreadful conditions. It later became a barracks and finally was used by Dublin Corporation for difficult tenants in its other housing schemes. It was demolished in 1975.

Marshalsea Lane

Poole Street

In 1785 there were five 'clothiers' living in Poole Street. The type of houses common in the district of Pimlico dated from the late 1600s.

The whole Liberties area was strongly affected by the decision of King Louis XIV of France to revoke the edict of Nantes in 1685, thus ending a century of tolerance of French Protestants. There thus followed an exodus of Huguenots to various parts of Britain and Ireland. Many settled in the Dublin Liberties, to which they brought their considerable skill as craftsmen and merchants. Sadly, by the end of the nineteenth century all that was left of their presence was their architecture, and that in a dreadfully decayed and dilapidated form. The modern terraced houses are standard local-authority issue and while they may be less picturesque than the old seventeenth-century houses, they are places where people can live in decency and dignity. It is easy to bewail the passing of 'old Dublin'. Indeed, a rather dubious industry has grown up around the concept of 'the rare old times'. Much of the so-called 'rare old times' was distinguished by squalor, poverty and public decay. Of all the changes in Dublin in the last ninety years, none has been more unambiguously good than the transformation in the provision of public housing.

Poole Street

Guinness' Brewery

Founded by Arthur Guinness in 1759, the brewery at St James's Gate is the largest in Europe. It is famed for the production of black, creamy-headed stout. The Guinness family have been involved in many acts of philanthropy and public munificence, immortalised in the Dubliners' exchange: 'The Guinnesses have been very good to the people of Dublin' – 'Ah but the people of Dublin have been very good to the Guinnesses'.

Guinness' has traditionally been the largest manufacturing employer in Dublin. At the turn of the century, they employed enormous numbers of coopers, farriers, draymen and other skilled and semi-skilled workers, not to mention casual labourers of one sort or another, all or most of whom have been gradually replaced as modern technological advances have transformed production and distribution. Despite all this, however, Guinness' had an enviable, indeed almost legendary, reputation as an employer. They offered secure, reasonably well-paid employment in good conditions to generations of Dubliners at times when the general run of Dublin employers were not exactly famed throughout the world for their benevolence. There have been a number of minor labour disputes in recent years in Guinness', but nothing of much consequence.

Most important of all, the product for which they are most famous remains as outstanding as ever. Guinness is truly one of the world's great drinks.

Guinness' Brewery

Grand Canal Harbour, Basin Lane

Until the early 1970s an arm of the Grand Canal ran from Kilmainham into the heart of Guinness' Brewery. Then it was filled in and although it has been remade as an attractive linear park, not all corners of the old basin have survived the change as happily.

The buildings in the background are among the few outstanding examples of Victorian industrial architecture in the city. They are the Guinness' buildings in Market Street, in the heart of the brewery area.

Grand Canal Harbour,
Basin Lane

Blackpitts

An area of Dublin's south inner city, its name is said to derive from mass plague graves. An alternative theory holds that the area was named after the fabric-dyeing industries in the area in the nineteenth century.

In common with the rest of the Liberties, Blackpitts shows great changes in the course of the twentieth century. Indeed, the areas of Dublin that have changed most are the poor, inner city districts and the outlying villages which have been absorbed into the city as suburbs.

Blackpitts

New Row

An old street in the heart of the Liberties, so called because it was an area situated just outside the medieval city walls and hence free from municipal rule – and taxes! Like most of the Liberties, little survives of New Row at the turn of the century, although the old warehouse on the right is still there, as is the great steeple of St Patrick's Cathedral in the background, picked out in the modern photograph by the superior camera technology of the 1980s.

New Row

St Catherine's Church, Thomas Street

St Catherine's Church was the site of the execution of Robert Emmet after the failed rebellion of 1803. He was hanged, drawn and quartered. When Thomas Street was widened in the 1960s some skeletons were discovered just outside St Catherine's. Thomas Street now has one of Dublin's last surviving street markets.

St Catherine's was built in the 1760s and commanded the view up the hill of Bridgefoot Street, a more significant vista then than now. It remains the dominant building in this part of Thomas Street, a street which for all its human activity is singularly undistinguished in its architecture. A church in honour of St Catherine has stood on this site since the late twelfth century. Although Thomas Street lies on the edge of the Liberties, it has not been physically transformed in the way many neighbouring streets have been. The basic elements are still in place, now as then.

St Catherine's Church,
Thomas Street

Parkgate, Parkgate Street

These main gates to the Phoenix Park were taken down to facilitate access to the Eucharistic Congress in 1932. In recent years there has begun a campaign to lessen the harmful effect of motorised transport on the flora and fauna of the Park. The traffic flow has been controlled and the erection of the gate piers was intended to help this. The actual gates, after some searching around the country, have recently been discovered and it is hoped to rehang them in the near future.

Despite the chopping and changing with the gate piers this corner of the city has remained relatively unchanged over the years. The retaining wall of the Phoenix Park, which runs west for the whole length of Conyngham Road and Chapelizod Road, has helped in this regard. Even in Parkgate Street itself, which connects Parkgate to the Liffey quays, there has been relatively little change over the years. One particularly fine survivor from the nineteenth century is Ryan's Pub, whose superb Victorian mahogany fittings are almost as justly famed as the excellence of its draught Guinness.

Parkgate, Parkgate Street

Phoenix Monument, Phoenix Park

Erected in 1747 by the Viceroy, Lord Chesterfield, it was originally situated at the centre of the crossroads. The monument was moved to its present site to facilitate motor racing in the 1930s. Nearby is an entrance gate to Aras an Uachtarain.

The fact that the Phoenix Monument was moved to make room for racing cars is a neat symbol of the largest single force for change in the Park in this century. The huge increase in the numbers of private cars, together with the spread of the western suburbs, has made the Park's main road a major commuter artery. As a result, the Phoenix Monument is likely to remain in its present unostentatious position.

Phoenix Monument,
Phoenix Park

Aras an Uachtarain

The Viceregal Lodge was home to the British viceroys who represented the monarch in Dublin. After the foundation of the Irish Free State in 1922 it was the residence of the Governor Generals of Ireland and in 1939 became Aras an Uachtarain, the home of the President of Ireland.

The Viceregal Lodge was built in 1751 as a home for one Nathaniel Clements, the chief ranger of the Phoenix Park. It was only in 1782 that it was bought by the government as a residence for the lord lieutenant, whereupon the original building was much extended and the portico was added so that the building assumed its modern appearance. The wings and the portico were the work of Francis Johnston, one of the most famous of all Dublin architects. For all its pretensions to grandeur, it remains a pretty unprepossessing building, perhaps an appropriate symbol for the whole viceregal presence in Dublin in the days of British rule.

Aras an Uachtarain

Mater Hospital

The Mater opened in 1861, having been nine years a-building. It was part of the huge institutional advance of the Catholic Church in Ireland in the nineteenth century. The foundress of the Sisters of Mercy, Catherine McAuley, had long dreamed of a hospital such as this. It quickly proved its worth in the 1866 cholera epidemic when it was the main centre of treatment for the north side of the city.

In Joyce's *Ulysses*, Leopold Bloom is treated in the Mater Misericordiae for a bee sting. Bloom lived further down Eccles Street at No. 7, a three-storey house demolished in the 1960s and now the site of the Mater Private Hospital. The door of No. 7 was salvaged and now resides in the Bailey public house in Duke Street.

Mater Hospital

Glasnevin Cemetery

The first interment here was a Michael Carey of
Francis Street on 22 February 1832. The 168 and a half
foot high round tower was erected in memory of
Daniel O'Connell who is buried at its base. It was here
that Paddy Dignam's funeral ended up in *Ulysses* on
its journey from his house in Newbridge Avenue,
Sandymount.

There are few enough places in Dublin which, in
their outward appearances at least, have hardly
changed at all in the course of the twentieth century.
Glasnevin Cemetery is one such. In particular, the
area just inside the main gate must appear now very
much as it did eighty or ninety years ago: the
mortuary chapel, the mausoleums of Catholic
archbishops of Dublin and the older plots – many of
them undisturbed for years – which are, naturally,
clustered at this end of the cemetery.

Glasnevin Cemetery

Chapelizod

Still retaining its village atmosphere, it can claim connections with the wider worlds of newspapers and literature. Alfred Lord Harmsworth, the founder of the *Daily Mail,* was born here in 1865. Joseph Sheridan Le Fanu also spent his childhood in Chapelizod – both he and Harmsworth's father were teachers in the Royal Hibernian schools in the Phoenix Park. The foreground of the modern photograph shows the new dual carriageway to the West under construction.

There was a walled town here as early as the thirteenth century and traditionally the village was associated with the harnessing of the river for milling as well as for salmon fishing. In the early seventeenth century Lord Valentia built a fine country house at Chapelizod which after the Restoration of 1660 became for a while the Viceregal Lodge. It was, of course, superseded by the present Aras an Uachtarain in the mid eighteenth century. King William III stayed there for some days after his victory at the Battle of the Boyne. For many years, particularly in the eighteenth century, Chapelizod was celebrated for its taverns, being at a convenient distance from the city without being part of it. It is perhaps appropriate, therefore, that Joyce used the Mullingar House as the setting for *Finnegans Wake*. Chapelizod has another Joycean connection. In one of the stories from *Dubliners*, 'A Painful Case' the protagonist, Mr James Duffy 'lived in Chapelizod because he wished to live as far as possible from the city of which he was a citizen and because he found all other suburbs of Dublin mean, modern, and pretentious'.

Chapelizod

Howth

The view from Howth Head north to Ireland's Eye is among the most spectacular to be found in Dublin. It was here 'among the rhododendrons' that Leopold Bloom proposed to Molly. Howth was also the scene of an important episode in Irish history when Erskine Childers' yacht *Asgard* landed 900 rifles there in July 1914. The village has retained much of its old-world charm and fishing is still an important aspect of the local economy.

Howth Castle has been in the possession of the St Lawrence family since the twelfth century. At the time of the Norman settlement, Howth was in the hands of the Danes. But Sir Almeric Tristram defeated the Danes here on 10 August 1177. Since it was the feast of St Laurence, Tristram took the surname of St Lawrence in thanksgiving for his victory, a family name which happily has survived in Howth Castle to this day.

Howth

Baldoyle

The village of Baldoyle – seven miles from the city centre – was synonymous for many years with horse racing, which took place at the racecourse which is behind the photographer on the left. The course opened in 1842 and closed in 1972. The 1931 World Cross-Country Championships were held here and won by Tim Smyth from Co Clare. The church in the photograph was built in 1836 by Reverend William Young.

Despite its significantly changed appearance, Baldoyle still retains a semi-rural feeling. It stands at the north-east extremity of the city proper, on the edge of the green belt that separates Dublin from Malahide and Portmarnock. Moreover, it is not on the main road to either of those places, but rather on the connecting back road from Howth and Sutton. So from being a satellite village of Dublin at the turn of the century, it has now graduated to being a suburb, but one with that strange, world's end atmosphere that one associates with the point where the city and the countryside melt into one another.

Baldoyle

Main Street, Swords

Swords, not so long ago a remote market village, is now the centre of a sprawling satellite town. The name has nothing to do with weaponry, but is named after a well *(sord)* dedicated to St Columcille. The castle (just visible above the houses at the end of the street), was the episcopal palace of the first Norman archbishop of Dublin, John Comyn, and the residence for all archbishops of the diocese until 1327 when they moved to Tallaght.

Main Street, Swords

Skerries

A coastal village which in years gone by was a popular resort for the Dublin professional classes who maintained holiday homes there.

Skerries lies in the heart of North County Dublin, a flat and fertile market gardening region which, despite its proximity to the capital, has maintained both its rural ways and its own distinctive personality. It was, and still remains, the only area in the Republic where cricket is one of the truly popular sports, with a whole network of clubs strung out across the North County, some of them dating back to the 1880s!

Skerries remains a popular seaside resort in the summer. These days, it is more a haunt for day-trippers, for improved roads and private and public transport has made it easily accessible from the city. Indeed, there has been a lot of housing development in the area as well, and Skerries is now in effect a commuter village for Dublin. It has, therefore, shared roughly the same fate as the outer suburban villages of Dublin for, although not a suburb of the city *per se*, its social development has followed a broadly similar course.

Skerries

Irishtown

Whence *'Al maner of men of Iryshe blode and women'* must have found their way when an order of King Henry VI made them quit the city of Dublin in 1454. At that time Irishtown was a collection of sandy hills cut off from the city by marshes, the river Dodder and the sea.

By 1660, Irishtown was listed in official records as having a population of ninety-eight, of whom twenty-three were of English descent and seventy-five of Irish descent. It was then not much more than an adjunct of Ringsend which, until the building of the South Wall and the consequent deepening of the Liffey channel in the eighteenth century, was the nearest deepwater berthage for ships calling to Dublin. As Ringsend's fortunes declined towards the end of the eighteenth century, those of Sandymount – on the other side of Ringsend – began to rise. To this day, Irishtown remains a small, but significantly distinct, half-way house between working-class Ringsend and middle-class Sandymount.

Irishtown

Sandymount

At first, horse trams worked the Sandymount route. Horse trams started in 1872, were electrified in 1896 and were phased out in 1932. The criss-cross patterns in the roadway were made of black Dublin Calp and were kept scrupulously clean of the horse dung which played havoc with the long dresses ladies wore at the time. The single decker tram in the distance travelled the route under the bridge at Bath Avenue. The single decker CIE bus, No. 52, was withdrawn from service in 1986.

Considering its proximity to the city, Sandymount was developed rather later than one might expect. Until the early eighteenth century there was nothing in this area except a herring fishery, but then a brickworks was established here. A small village grew up around the works called Brickfield Town near which there was a celebrated inn, kept by one Johnny Maclean, with the quaint name of the Conniving House. The brickworks eventually fell into decay but the village gradually evolved into modern Sandymount in the early nineteenth century. It quickly became a settled, middle-class suburb. Its stability is evident from these photographs, which demonstrate the surprisingly small level of physical change in the course of the present century.

Sandymount

Blackrock Park

There were several pleasure gardens in Dublin in the late eighteenth and early nineteenth centuries. The Rotunda, Coburg and Ranelagh gardens provided this sort of entertainment for the citizens of the city and suburbs. On grounds formerly owned by Lord Lisle in Blackrock, a park called Vauxhall Gardens was opened in 1793. This had a short existence, ending in 1804, but was reopened once more in 1873.

Blackrock Park

Blackrock Village

The elegant Victorian village of Blackrock has changed little save for the curtailment of traffic – which can no longer go south on the right of the picture – and the perambulations of the tenth-century stone cross on the right of the modern picture. The cross, which was used by the Dublin Corporation as a boundary marker, stood somewhere to the rear of the horse-drawn carriage. In 1959 it was moved to the right to facilitate road-widening and in recent years moved once more onto the plinth pictured.

Little is known about Blackrock until the eighteenth century when it became a favourite seaside resort for Dublin people. As a consequence Blackrock, like Chapelizod, became famous for the volume of intoxicating drink consumed there. At least one pub, The Three Tun, still survives in the village, in name at least, from the eighteenth century. Blackrock's eighteenth-century popularity was helped in no small degree by the fact that both the lord lieutenant and the archbishop of Dublin had villas nearby. In the nineteenth century, the railway transformed Blackrock from a country watering place into a commuter suburb for the well-to-do. Broadly speaking, that is the position it holds today. As these photographs demonstrate, the homely, largely Victorian character of its main street has been little changed over the years.

Blackrock Village

Seapoint

There are twenty-one Martello Towers around Dublin, stretching from Bray to Balbriggan. Once intended to defend Ireland from the threat of Napoleonic invasion, they now serve many purposes, ranging from homes to museums. Sadly, some are derelict. This one was used in the 1890s to advertise Austin & Co., an importer of French and other foreign fancy goods who had premises at 37 Westmoreland Street. Seapoint railway station was opened in 1863. The modern DART train service was opened in 1984.

Seapoint

Church of St Mary, Monkstown

Built around an earlier church in 1785, this exotic concoction by John Semple features a 'chessman' exterior, just one of its unique architectural features. The parabolic vault is another, though not as impressive as that in the Black Church, Mountjoy Street, also by Semple. The ladder in the middle of the road was for the use of the fire service.

Church of St Mary,
Monkstown

Monkstown

The monks, from whom the name Monkstown derives, were Cistercians who built Monkstown Castle in the twelfth century. They were farmers and fishermen and after the dissolution of the monasteries their lands were granted to Sir John Travers, Master of Ordnance of Ireland.

Monkstown as we know it today is part of the development of the coastline to the south-east of the city, from Merrion to Dalkey and Killiney, as middle-class and upper middle-class suburbs. This development was, of course, greatly facilitated by the development of the Dublin and Kingstown railway in the 1830s.

Monkstown

Peoples' Park, Dun Laoghaire

The easy availability of local granite led to the opening of several quarries in the area of Dun Laoghaire. The pond in Moran Park was one such – the site of the Peoples' Park was another. This quarry was filled and opened as a park in 1890.

Peoples' Park,
Dun Laoghaire

Town Hall, Dun Laoghaire

Built in the style of a Venetian palace, the Town Hall was erected in the late 1870s. Its 120 feet high tower, with that of St Michael's Church, dominates the skyline for the incoming ferry passengers. In the foreground is the entrance and part of the Peoples' Pavilion, built in 1903. The all white wooden building had almost the appearance of a giant Mississippi riverboat. There were concerts, bowling greens and tea rooms in the beautifully kept grounds. The Pavilion was destroyed in a disastrous fire in 1915. Though the railway had come to Kingstown in 1834, there was local opposition to it coming into the town. The original terminus was at the West Pier.

Dun Laoghaire used to be known in an anglicised form as Dunleary but was renamed Kingstown in 1821 to celebrate the visit to Ireland of King George IV. The king was to have put ashore here, but he was so drunk on arrival that it was thought unseemly to expose him to the crowds in this condition, so his yacht berthed instead in Howth and allowed his majesty to sneak in the back way. He did, however, depart from Dunleary which was renamed Kingstown in his honour. This time, it seems, he was sober.

Dunleary had been a fishing village for many centuries before the first pier was built in the 1750s but it was not until the arrival of the railway in 1834 that it developed fully as a terminus for cross-channel passenger ships. This in turn led to its development first as a satellite town and now effectively as an outer suburb of Dublin.

Town Hall, Dun Laoghaire

Dun Laoghaire Harbour

Dun Laoghaire was named after a fort (Dun) built by Laoghaire, King of Tara, in the fifth century. The name was changed to Kingstown in 1821 on the visit of King George IV, but reverted to its old name during the War of Independence in 1920. The harbour was constructed between 1817 and 1821, the two imposing piers enclosing 250 acres of water. In 1826 the steam packet service was transferred from Howth to Kingstown and today it is the main passenger ferry port in the Republic.

One of the most celebrated incidents in the history of the harbour took place on 31 March 1908. Two rival companies, the City of Dublin Steam Packet Company and the London and North Western Railway Company, ran steam packet ships on the cross-channel route. Traditionally the City of Dublin berthed at Dun Laoghaire and the L&NWR at North Wall. However, the L&NWR had sought a berthage at Dun Laoghaire for some time and in the spring of 1908 they got it. In response the City of Dublin Company saw to it that three of its mailboats were tied up in the harbour upon the arrival of the first L&NWR ship, thus occupying all the available berthages. This farcical display went down in history as the Battle of the Pier. By an odd coincidence it was repeated, after a fashion, seventy-four years later, in March 1982 when the B&I Line — which had traditionally been excluded from Dun Laoghaire – found that its arrival there caused local industrial action. The crew of the B&I's *MV Munster* then sailed her into the mouth of the harbour, thus blocking the entrance to the incoming Sealink ship *St David*.

Dun Laoghaire Harbour

Dalkey (Main Street)

In the eighty years or more since the old photograph was taken, there have been few alterations to the streetscape. The town hall was one of seven castles which defended the medieval port – which up to the end of the sixteenth century was the only safe deep water berthage for large ships near Dublin. The large ships there unloaded their cargoes onto smaller boats which could navigate the sandy shallows of the Liffey.

Dalkey declined from the end of the sixteenth century, as Ringsend developed. From then until the nineteenth century, the area fell on hard times commercially but was still the location of a number of substantial houses. One of the eighteenth-century residents was Peter Wilson, a bookseller and the publisher of the *Dublin Almanac*. He wrote that in 1770 the village consisted of the ruins of the castles and the church, some good houses and about twenty cabins which 'served indiscriminately for the owners, the cattle and their swine'. Charlotte Brooke, the author of *Reliques of Irish Poetry* (1790) also lived in Dalkey.

Modern Dalkey is, like most of the surrounding area, a product of nineteenth-century middle-class development along the line of the railway. Like so many other such areas from Sandymount out, it has maintained a remarkable stability both in its physical appearance and in its social structure.

Dalkey (Main Street)

The Convent, Dalkey

This impressive nineteenth-century building on the coast is the Loreto Abbey. It houses both primary and secondary schools run by the Loreto sisters.

The Loreto Order was founded in Dublin by Frances Ball, a wealthy woman of charitable disposition, in 1821. In that year, the Order opened in Rathfarnham the first of their schools for the education of middle-class Catholic girls, a task which it continues to perform to this day. The Dalkey convent was founded in 1843.

The Convent, Dalkey

Dalkey Hill

Dalkey is a picturesque village on the coast, south of the city. The bay is reputed to resemble Naples, hence the Italian influence evident in place names such as Vico Road and Sorrento Terrace. The bandstand in the picture is a setting in Hugh Leonard's play 'A Life'.

Dalkey Hill

Ballybrack

There are several imposing private residences right on the shore at Strand Road. The two most imposing are pictured here, their twin towers mirroring the military fortifications of the nearby Martello Tower.

Ballybrack's development echoes that of other adjacent areas in this part of Co Dublin. However, it is less thoroughly built up than other suburbs and some hints of the more spacious and relaxed atmosphere of prosperous late-Victorian Dublin are visible here.

Ballybrack

Tallaght Church

The nineteenth-century St Maelrun's parish stands on the site of the original monastery of the eighth-century saint. The bell tower *(left)* is all that remains of the medieval parish church. The first modern war correspondent, William Russell who reported the Crimean War for *The Times* of London, was born in Tallaght in 1820.

Tallaght Church stands in the middle of one of the most changed landscapes in twentieth-century Ireland. Even in the 1960s, Tallaght was still a small village on the edge of Dublin, separated from the outer suburbs by a narrow green belt. But the enormous expansion of housing in the area, which resulted in the creation of a new town the size of Limerick, has swept away nearly all traces of the old life.

Tallaght Church

Inchicore

The Oblate Fathers arrived in Inchicore in 1856 and with the help of workers from the Great Southern & Western Railway who worked nearby, erected a wooden church in four days! The present chapel was built twenty-two years later. Note that in the Lawrence Collection photograph both spires have not yet reached their present height. Note also that the statue has been rotated 90°!

In the eighteenth century Inchicore was a rural area well outside the city limits and the site of the family house of the Lords Annesley. In the nineteenth century, however, the coming of the railway transformed everything. The building of the railway works created a demand for skilled labour and resulted in the influx of many craftsmen into the area. The railway also built a small estate of houses for its workers in a style typical of the artisan dwellings built by railway companies for their workers in the late nineteenth century. They remain a pleasing, if relatively hidden, feature of an area which is otherwise among the least attractive in the city. Added to the general shabbiness of its appearance, Inchicore has a bad traffic problem since all the traffic, both private and commercial, for the south and south-west is funnelled along its narrow main street.

Inchicore

Terenure Crossroads

Two types of tram served this area. The Blessington steam tram, which operated from 1888 to 1933, had its terminus where the old Classic cinema stood. The electric trams displaced the horse trams from 1896 and the identity of the vehicles in the picture can be ascertained by the shape of the shield sticking up at the front, a necessary device in an era of widespread illiteracy. The triangle marked the Terenure route and the Maltese Cross that for Rathfarnham.

Terenure was very much a peripheral village, hardly even a suburb as such, at the turn of the century. The last ninety years have, of course, seen the relentless march of the city outwards in all possible directions, transforming Terenure and many other districts like it into conventional residential suburbs.

Terenure Crossroads

Rathmines

Rathmines, which was made an independent township in 1847, had its own waterworks, Town Hall and technical schools. It ceased to have autonomous township status when it was absorbed into Dublin in 1930.

The name Rathmines derives from the fact that in medieval times the district contained a rath on property which came into the possession of a family called de Meones. In 1649 a royalist army under the Duke of Ormond was routed by parliamentary troops under Colonel Michael Jones in what became known as the Battle of Rathmines. In the eighteenth century, the area passed into the ownership of Lords Palmerston, whose names survive in some of the street names to this day. The district retained its rural character until the nineteenth century when, along with Rathgar, it was developed as one of Dublin's early suburbs.

Because it had independent township status it was able to levy lower rates on its residents than the Dublin Corporation. Like many of the other independent townships, it thus became a haven for well-to-do people fleeing from what they regarded as penal rates of local taxation. An alternative view of this development might see nineteenth-century Rathmines as a ghetto for a Dublin middle class which declined to pull its financial weight in the city and whose parsimony deprived Dublin Corporation of revenues which could well have been applied to the relief of the appalling social conditions then prevailing in the city centre.

Rathmines

Ballsbridge

The Ball in question is thought to be a man who owned property in the area. The present bridge is the third on this site; the first was built in 1791; it was rebuilt in 1835 and again in 1904. The building on the far bank in the right-hand corner was the Pembroke District Town Hall and is now headquarters of the City of Dublin VEC.

Ballsbridge